FAMOUS MOVIE MONSTERS™

INTRODUCING

ZOMBIES

The Rosen Publishing Group, Inc.,
New York

THOMAS FORGET

*To the staff of Harris Public Library
in Woonsocket, RI*

Published in 2007 by The Rosen Publishing Group, Inc.
29 East 21st Street, New York, NY 10010

First Edition

Library of Congress Cataloging-in-Publication Data

Forget, Thomas.
Introducing Zombies/Thomas Forget.
   p. cm.—(Famous movie monsters)
Filmography: p.
Includes bibliographical references and index.
ISBN 1-4042-0852-6 (lib. bndg.)
1. Zombie films—History and criticism. I. Title: Zombies.
II. Title. III. Series.
PN1995.9.Z63F67 2006
791.43'6375—dc22

                                          2005032019

Manufactured in Malaysia

On the Cover: Decaying zombies look for food in *Zombie (1979),* by Italian director Lucio Fulci.

CONTENTS

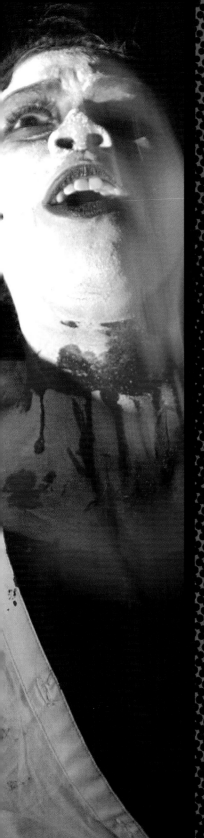

CHAPTER 1

NIGHT OF THE LIVING DEAD

Siblings Johnny and Barbara arrive at a quiet, rural cemetery to place a wreath on their father's grave. Dusk has fallen, and while Barbara is respectful and a little afraid, Johnny is in a testy mood from the long drive. As distant thunder cracks and the sun continues to sink, they start bickering. Johnny begins making fun of his sister's fear, saying "They're coming to get you, Barbara!" in a low, creepy voice.

Although Johnny is only joking, Barbara is becoming genuinely frightened. Her fear increases as a stranger begins staggering toward them. Johnny continues to kid Barbara, saying, "Look! There comes one of them now!" The stranger, who is now quite close to the siblings, suddenly lunges at Barbara, tearing at her jacket and trying to pull her closer. His pale face shows only one thing: hunger!

Johnny rushes to his sister's defense, but the large man quickly overpowers him. The man throws Johnny to the ground, smashing

Johnny (Russell Streiner) struggles with *Night of the Living Dead*'s first zombie (Bill Hinzman), as his sister, Barbara (Judith O'Dea), scrambles away. Besides playing Johnny, Streiner was also a producer of the film. Because of the movie's low budget, many of the actors cast in *Night of the Living Dead* were friends of the filmmakers.

his head on a gravestone. The crazed stranger turns toward Barbara, who runs toward the car. With the maniac in hot pursuit, she enters the car, only to discover that she doesn't have the keys. It seems there is no escape from the determined, silent man, as he finally picks up a brick and smashes the window.

Avoiding his grasp, Barbara puts the car in neutral and it rolls away from the attacker. Unfortunately, she crashes the car into a tree and has to escape on foot to an abandoned farmhouse.

Barbara locks herself in the house, breathing a momentary sigh of relief. As she explores the house, she is horrified to discover that its lone occupant is a rotting corpse! The phones don't work, and the mysterious stranger is still outside, joined now by other staggering people in torn clothing.

In shock, Barbara attempts to flee the house. As soon as she steps outside, a car's headlights greet her. A lone man jumps out of the car and pulls Barbara inside to safety. His name is Ben and he's a traveler. He tries in vain to comfort Barbara, but she is terrified beyond reason. Ben does his best to remain calm and starts making plans to insure their safety. Noticing that there are more and more of the staggering people approaching the house, Ben goes on the attack. He assaults the creatures with a tire iron and discovers that bashing in their heads is one of the only things that seems to stop them.

Returning indoors, Ben begins the business of fortifying the house. It's tiring work, and Barbara is in no shape to help him, but Ben is determined. As he goes about boarding up the doors and windows, he explains what little he knows about the strange people outside to the silent Barbara. He also tells her how he survived an attack by the madmen at the local diner.

Barbara tells her own story and begs Ben to go back outside to rescue her brother. Ben tries to explain that they will be killed if they leave the house, but Barbara is hysterical and won't listen to reason. Ben is forced to knock her unconscious for her own good. While she sleeps, he finishes boarding up and listens to the radio. Amazingly, it seems that the authorities know just as little as Ben does. Nobody is sure why some individuals have become mindless killers, but the phenomenon has spread all over the country. Luckily for Ben, he finds a gun and some bullets in the house.

As the radio continues to broadcast information, Ben learns that the murderers are eating the people they kill! On the heels of this shocking announcement, a door opens in the house, startling the recently awakened Barbara. Ben rushes to see what is causing the commotion and finds two men. They explain that they've been in the basement the whole time with three other people. Ben, furious that they didn't come help him board up,

Ben (Duane Jones) uses fire to keep zombies away from the front porch of the house where he has taken refuge. Ben learned during his escape from a diner that fire is one of the only things that will keep the mindless zombies away. It is also one of the only sure ways to fully destroy a zombie's body.

immediately begins arguing with the older man, Harry Cooper.

Mr. Cooper insists that the basement is the safest place to be, but Ben disagrees. After some back-and-forth, Ben manages to convince the younger man, Tom, to stay upstairs with him. He also demands that he keep the radio. Tom gets his girlfriend, Judy, from the basement, leaving Mr. Cooper to sulk downstairs with his wife and daughter. His daughter, Karen, has been bitten by one of the strange people outside and is very sick.

Helen Cooper argues with her husband about his decision to stay in the basement. He finally gives in, and they move upstairs with everyone else. A recently discovered television set reveals more shocking information. Not only have the killers been eating their victims, but recently deceased people seem to be rising from the dead, becoming cannibal creatures themselves.

The television news also reports that there is a strong suspicion that a crashed Venus space probe leaking radiation may be the cause of the living dead assault, but they aren't sure. No one, it seems, really knows why the dead are hunting the living. The news report also reveals that people who have been bitten by the dead are infected with a virus and will inevitably change into fiendish flesh-eaters themselves. Karen is already beginning to show signs that she has been infected with the virus.

The government has organized relief centers, one of which is not far from the farmhouse. Ben concocts a daring plan to escape to safety. Using keys found in the basement of the house, he and Tom will try to unlock the farm's gas pump to get gas for the truck parked outside. If they can get the truck running, they can drive to the relief station. They gather supplies to make firebombs and set out, with a frightened Judy as a last-minute addition. They are able to get to the gas pump, but in a split second, everything goes wrong. The truck catches fire as Tom and Judy try to drive it away. As they struggle to get free, the truck explodes. The group's only chance to escape has vanished.

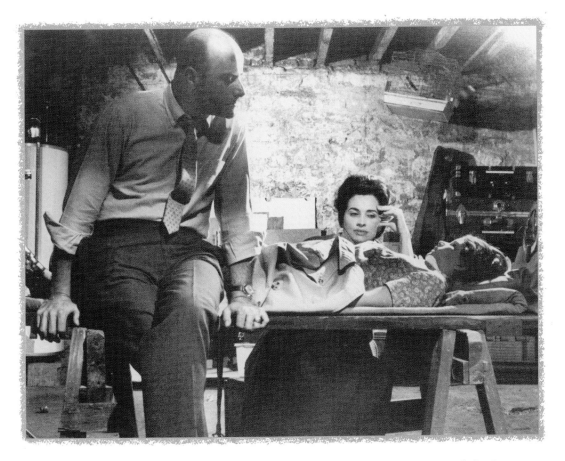

Karen Cooper (Kyra Schon) rests on a makeshift table in the basement of the house. Mr. and Mrs. Cooper (Karl Hardman and Marilyn Eastman) check to see how she is feeling. They'll soon find out that their daughter is infected with a very dangerous virus, a virus that will leave her hungry for human flesh.

Ben now finds himself alone outside, armed with only a torch, surrounded by living dead. As he bravely struggles back to the house, he finds that Harry Cooper has locked him out. With the dead bearing down on him, he's forced to kick the door open. As soon as he and Mr. Cooper finish boarding up the door, Ben attacks him. While the survivors fight among

In this scene, a group of zombies recoil from a fire set by the survivors. Though fire works to keep the zombies away for a time, the survivors are eventually over- whelmed by the sheer number of zombies who show up at their doorstep. The living dead are relentless—they never get tired and never need sleep.

themselves, the hungry dead help themselves to a grim feast of what is left of Tom and Judy.

Inside the house, the survivors gather to watch another emergency broadcast. They learn that well-armed posses have assembled to hunt the dead all over the countryside. It seems that there is still hope of a rescue. Unfortunately, the power in the house suddenly goes out. The terrified survivors are now without light or news from the outside world and are left with only one rifle as defense.

Now that the house has gone dark, the dead begin their final assault. They hammer at the boards on the windows, relentlessly clawing their way into the house. As Ben rushes to the nearest window to beat them back, he drops the rifle. Mr. Cooper, who has been waiting for this moment, rushes in to grab it. Finally, he has the control he wanted. Cooper is through taking orders. Aiming the gun at Ben, he orders his wife down into the basement.

Ben knows that the deranged Cooper is beyond reasoning. He hurls a board at Cooper and wrestles the gun away. As Cooper struggles to get up from the floor, Ben levels the rifle at him and coolly fires. Stunned, Cooper grabs his belly and totters down the basement stairs. In the meantime, the ghouls have made headway and are clawing at the defenseless Helen Cooper. Barbara rushes to Helen's aid but finds herself in the clutches of the dead as well.

With Barbara taking the creatures' attention, Helen Cooper follows her wounded husband down into the basement. Instead of finding shelter, however, she stumbles upon the most gruesome scene imaginable. Her young daughter, Karen, has become a flesh-eater. As Mrs. Cooper reels in shock, Karen turns her attention from her meal. She has been eating Mr. Cooper, her own father!

Helen tries to reason with Karen as the girl advances toward her, but there is nothing left of the daughter she once knew. All that shows on her blood-stained face is naked hunger. Karen picks up a garden trowel and savagely plunges it into her mother over and over again. The cruel truth of this night of the living dead is that anyone can become your worst enemy, even your own flesh and blood!

Upstairs, the living dead have broken into the house. As Ben and Barbara try to defend themselves from the onslaught of the dead, Barbara is shocked to be confronted by a familiar-looking corpse. Her brother Johnny, now one of the living dead, begins advancing toward her. There is no recognition in his eyes. Barbara screams at him, but Johnny carries her away on a tide of hungry, clawing bodies. Ben now stands alone.

Barely escaping several grasping hands, Ben frantically fights his way past Karen and makes his way to the basement. The battle for the farmhouse is over, and the living have lost. Corpses flood the house and wander around looking for victims, their eyes blank.

Defeated, Ben slumps down in the basement. He quickly shoots Mr. and Mrs. Cooper as they rise from the dead. After an entire night of trying to stay in control, Ben finally loses it, smashing things and putting his head in his hands. There is nothing left for him to do but wait until someone comes to help. Upstairs, a bizarre party of the dead streams through the empty house.

As dawn breaks, hunting parties comb the countryside, searching for the living dead. Armed posses appear to have finally gotten the living dead infestation under control. In the farmhouse basement, Ben hears the gunshots of the hunters and cautiously makes his way upstairs. Peering through the window, he sees that the rescue he's been waiting for is finally here.

Outside, the hunters continue to do away with the living dead. One hunter spies some movement in the farmhouse, takes aim, and fires, scoring a direct hit. His target, unfortunately, is Ben, who hits the floor, dead. After surviving an army of undead killers, it's a foolish hunter's mistake that does Ben in. This night of the living dead leaves no survivors to tell the tale.

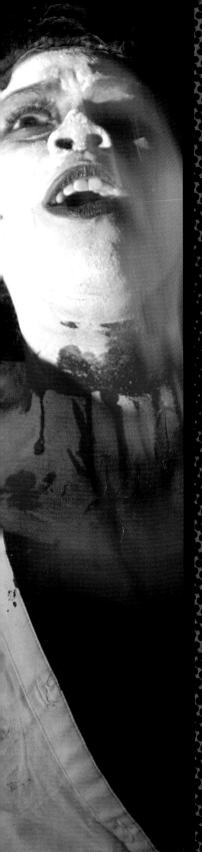

CHAPTER 2

RAISING THE DEAD

Night of the Living Dead was not filmed in glamorous Hollywood but in the blue-collar steel town of Pittsburgh, Pennsylvania. A group of friends, including George Romero, Russell Streiner, Gary Streiner, and John Russo ran a small film production company called The Latent Image. Founded in 1961, The Latent Image, Inc., had a good reputation for doing high-quality work on a small budget. They completed many successful local commercials but found that advertising agencies were unwilling to give them big accounts. The Latent Image was winning awards, but the men running it were barely able to pay their rent.

All of this was particularly frustrating for Romero. Born and raised in New York City, George Romero was a talented painter and sculptor, but film was in his blood. He had worked as a production assistant on the film *Bell, Book, and Candle*, starring Jimmy Stewart, Kim Novak, and Ernie Kovacs. He met the rest of his partners in The Latent Image while studying art at Pittsburgh's Carnegie Institute of Technology (now Carnegie-Mellon University).

Commercials paid their rent and helped them hone their filmmaking skills, but the men of The Latent Image wanted something more. Although their company was small, they had big dreams. They wanted to make a feature film. At a lunch meeting in January 1967, John Russo and George Romero started cooking up a plan.

A TEAM EFFORT

By 1967, The Latent Image team was fully equipped to make a feature film, but they didn't have the money they needed. They had looked for funding in the straight-laced Pittsburgh financial community, but as Romero recalls in John Russo's *The Complete Night of the Living Dead Film Book*, "Pittsburgh money feels safe investing in iron foundries. You tell them you want to make a film, they want to beat you over the head and put you in a straight-jacket."

John Russo came up with an ingenious money-raising idea. He suggested that, rather than finding one investor to put up a lot of money, they find ten investors to contribute $600 each. They had done a short comedy film a few years before for $2,000, so they figured $6,000 would be enough to get them started on a full-length feature.

Once they had the ball rolling on funding, they had to decide what kind of film they wanted to make. Figuring that they could easily make a scarier film than other filmmakers, they decided to make a monster movie. At the time, drive-in movie theaters all over the country were attracting teenagers in droves, and horror pictures were some of the most popular attractions. Their small budget demanded that their monster picture take place in the present day, to avoid spending money on period sets and costumes.

They also needed more money than the original $6,000. In order to open things up to other investors, they formed a company called Image Ten, Inc., for the sole purpose of making the movie. Image Ten, Inc., offered investors stock in their feature film. When all was said and done, they had raised $60,000 and managed to get loans for the rest. *Night of the Living Dead* cost, in total, $114,000—a microscopic amount, even in 1968.

THE MANY FACES OF *NIGHT OF THE LIVING DEAD*

Although the concept behind *Night of the Living Dead* is a simple one, it was not the first idea the company came up with. Their original story concept was for a horror comedy about young aliens who befriend some teenagers on Earth. They were forced to scrap that idea because they couldn't afford the special effects. The second idea they worked with was closer to the finished product. This featured a group of aliens or ghouls keeping corpses under glass to use as food.

After a lull in activity, George Romero showed up one day with a forty-page short story. The story, inspired by Richard Matheson's 1954 novel, *I Am Legend*, dealt with humans under assault by living corpses.

The story marked perhaps the first time that zombies were portrayed as undead cannibals. Up until then, onscreen zombies in films such as *White Zombie* (1932) were generally humans in trances under the control of a voodoo master or scientist. Everyone at The Latent Image liked Romero's dark horror

George Romero sits among the tools that have made him an acclaimed director of horror films. The son of a movie-poster artist from New York, filmmaking is in Romero's blood. Before hitting it big with *Night of the Living Dead*, he was an award-winning director of advertisements in Pittsburgh, Pennsylvania.

drama, and John Russo worked on a script based on the story. The script didn't differ much from what Romero had written, but one major change would mark the film as a true original. Unlike almost every other horror picture ever made, in this one, there would be no survivors.

While an early draft of the script had Barbara survive the night by hiding in the basement, they decided that it would be more terrifying if the movie contained no hope whatsoever. As Romero explains in John Russo's *The Complete Night of the Living Dead Film Book*: "The film opens with a situation that has already disintegrated to a point of little hope, and it moves progressively toward absolute despair and ultimate tragedy. Nobody comes riding in at the end with the secret formula that will save us all." This bleak attitude set *Night of the Living Dead* apart from its competition.

PRODUCTION PITFALLS

Even though the script was finished, there were some big problems for the filmmakers to deal with. First of all, they had to contend with the weather. The script was completed just as an especially cold winter began. When they tried to begin filming, the camera's motors froze. They also desperately needed to find a farmhouse that would be suitable for filming. The catch was that, while the farmhouse needed to look habitable, they needed the freedom to destroy it. Unfortunately, they did not have the budget to build or purchase a farmhouse of their own.

During the winter, they worked hard casting the film. Most of the roles were given to investors and friends, although semi-professional actors were hired to play the most important roles. Perhaps most important was the casting of Ben, the closest thing the film has to a hero. Duane Jones was chosen for the part.

A skillful and charming actor, Jones added a depth to Ben that was not there in the script. Although Ben's ethnicity is not specified in the script, it would become a significant detail

Surrounded by hecklers, three civil rights activists attempt to receive equal service at a "whites only" lunch counter in Jackson, Mississippi, in 1963. Released the same year that civil rights leader Martin Luther King Jr. was assassinated, *Night of the Living Dead* was regarded by many as a political allegory for the civil rights movement. While it may not seem strange today that *Night of the Living Dead* featured an African American hero, this was an uncommon choice at the time.

of the film. Jones is African American and at this time it was rare for an African American to be cast as the heroic leading man in a film, especially in a horror film. *Night of the Living Dead* was released in the same year that civil rights leader Martin Luther King Jr. was assassinated, leading many people to believe that the film was intended to be interpreted politically.

A group of Romero's zombies stagger around in the daytime countryside in Pennsylvania. The filmmakers searched long and hard for a good place to film their movie. They needed to find a farmhouse that looked livable, but that they could also wreck. The house they found was to be bulldozed as soon as they were finished filming.

The filmmakers eventually found a great farmhouse in Evans City, Pennsylvania. Its owner was preparing to bulldoze it to make room for his crops, so it didn't matter whether or not the filmmakers damaged it. To make it seem livable, they built a working fireplace and filled the house with furniture purchased from thrift stores or donated by investors. By the time all of the work on the house was done, it was spring, and they were ready to film.

CUTTING CORNERS

By 1968, most movies were filmed in color, and color film could be very expensive. In order to save money, *Night of the Living Dead* was shot in black and white. This gave the film a stark, gritty look that was alien to most of the horror films being made at the time. Special effects were easier to accomplish without having to worry about creating realistic color. The fake blood in the movie, for instance, was actually chocolate syrup.

The filmmakers also saved money on production by taking advantage of any favors they could, such as the use of a local radio station's helicopter for aerial shots and animal parts donated by a local slaughterhouse. They found that the best way to keep from having to pay actors was for the investors themselves to play most of the roles. Although the investors were flattered to be offered parts in the film, it was hard work. A group of investors even had to live in the house (which lacked

NAMING THE FILM

Called Monster Flick throughout production, *Night of the Living Dead* didn't receive its final title until it was ready for release. Once the filmmakers had a finished 35-mm print, it was called *Night of the Flesh Eaters*, but because that was in use already by another production, they had to change it. The next title was *Night of Anubis*, a reference to the Egyptian god of death, but they rejected it for being too obscure. Naming the film *Night of the Living Dead* ended up being a last-minute decision.

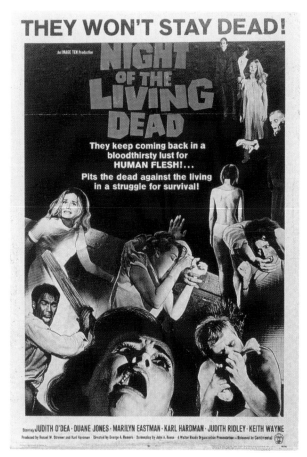

THEY WON'T STAY DEAD!

An IMAGE TEN Production

NIGHT OF THE LIVING DEAD

They keep coming back in a
bloodthirsty lust for
HUMAN FLESH!...

Pits the dead against the living
in a struggle for survival!

Starring JUDITH O'DEA · DUANE JONES · MARILYN EASTMAN · KARL HARDMAN · JUDITH RIDLEY · KEITH WAYNE
Produced by Russell W. Streiner and Karl Hardman · Directed by George A. Romero · Screenplay by John A. Russo · A Walter Reade Organization Presentation — Released by Continental

A collage of scenes from the film, the poster
for *Night of the Living Dead* shows the wide
variety of zombies that appear in the film.
Because the filmmakers figured people would
have died during all sorts of activities, some
of the zombies in the film are wearing suits
and others are in ripped clothing. One zombie
is even wearing a morgue sheet.

running water) while filming, as
the filmmakers could not afford a
security force to watch their cam-
eras and other equipment.

The filming of *Night of the
Living Dead* took about nine
months altogether. Shooting was
frequently interrupted as the The
Latent Image team filmed commercials in order to keep the business
afloat. When all of the rough
footage was completed, Romero
did all of the editing and cutting
himself, another important money-
saving method. When it came time
to make a finished 35-mm print of
the film, Russell Streiner made a
bargain with the president of a
film-developing company. If Streiner
could beat him at chess, the man
agreed to print the film for free.
Streiner won, and the president
printed the film at no cost, saving them almost $2,000.

SELLING THE DEAD

With the film finished and printed, the filmmakers now needed
to find a distributor. Although they were almost able to place

the film with Columbia, the big studio ultimately passed. They found distribution through Continental Pictures, a small company that usually did not do horror films.

The film premiered in their hometown of Pittsburgh. It was crucial to the film's success that it do well in Pittsburgh. The distributor would not spend the money to play it all over the country if it wasn't a hit in its first market. Since they couldn't count on their small distributor to advertise the movie in Pittsburgh, the investment group took things into their own hands, bombarding local newspapers with press releases. Even though their movie was small, they refused to treat it that way.

The premier was a smash. Everyone who was invited showed up, and the audience reaction was exactly what the filmmakers wanted. They were terrified! In the following weeks, showings of the movie all over Pittsburgh were packed. *Night of the Living Dead* was a hit. News of the movie spread like wildfire from city to city, and it sold out theaters wherever it played. Although *Night of the Living Dead* was extremely different from big Hollywood movies, it was on its way to becoming one of the classics of the horror genre.

While they didn't know it at the time, Romero and company had done something else: they reinvented the zombie. While no one in the movie ever actually calls the creatures "zombies," that was the name that caught on. After *Night of the Living Dead*, zombies would never be the same. What had been blank-eyed servants of voodoo masters were now rotting, ravenous, flesh-eating cannibals under the control of no one.

CHAPTER 3

ORIGINS OF THE DEAD

While the fantastic zombies of *Night of the Living Dead* are thankfully not real, zombies in film have their beginnings in real-life folklore. To date, there are no instances of living people rising from the grave to eat their fellow human beings, but stories of real-life walking dead exist in the religion of voodoo.

A voodoo priest, or houngan, is thought to have certain powers. One of these powers is the ability to possess a recently dead body and force it to do his bidding. In voodoo, the body is considered to still be a usable container once the soul has left it. With the proper rituals and potions, a houngan can use it for any purpose, good or evil. Zombies, if they ever truly existed, may have been used as workers on sugarcane plantations in Haiti. According to legend, zombies followed any order given to them and never grew tired or complained.

REAL-LIFE ZOMBIES

Stories of houngans controlling dead bodies must be taken with a grain of salt, but there have been several modern instances where dead people are thought to have been seen years later, with voodoo magic claimed as the cause. In 1985, an anthropologist named Wade Davis learned of a strange drug that was said to put people in a deep trance, effectively making them zombies. Davis went to Haiti to investigate the existence of the drug after hearing several stories about dead people walking around with the living.

In one case, a man named Clairvius Narcisse, who had been declared dead in 1962, had been found to be alive and well by the time of Davis's investigation. He claimed that he had been the victim of a voodoo cult that gave him a drug that made him appear dead. After his burial, the cult dug him up, beat him, and used him as a slave for two years. Davis believed that the effects of the "zombie drug," combined with regular beatings, would be enough to leave any person in a trancelike state.

Davis searched in vain for a houngan who would perform the zombification process on someone in front of him. The

The tomb of "Voodoo Queen" Marie Laveau in New Orleans, Louisiana. A legendary figure in eighteenth-century New Orleans, Laveau was known as a voodoo sorceress and had a great deal of influence in the city. Before her death, she reportedly converted back to Roman Catholicism, the religion she was born into.

priests wanted more money than Davis was willing to pay, and he had no real way of knowing whether the zombification was real or not. Despite all of his work in Haiti, he could not prove that real-life zombies or a zombie drug existed. Still, Davis had his theories. He believed that the zombie drug was a secret recipe passed down all the way from Africa from person to person and that a secret cult keeps the information away from the outside world.

Davis's experiments in Haiti became the basis for a book and movie, both called *The Serpent and the Rainbow*. The film, released in 1988, heavily dramatized the events of the book, and it was one of the first successful voodoo zombie films in a long time.

The zombies in traditional tales are not threatening or violent like the ones invented by Romero and company. While they can be forced to do evil by the person controlling them, the real terror in the Haitian zombie is that of becoming one, not being

THE LORD OF THE ZOMBIES

In voodoo folklore, the voodoo god of death is a man named Baron Samedi. Clothed in a black coat and top hat like an undertaker, he is the figure that a voodoo priest prays to while trying to make a zombie. There are some that believe that the baron may have been a real houngan many years ago and has become a legend. Translated from the French, his name means "Baron Saturday."

This painting by Hector Hyppolite depicts a cruel voodoo master creating zombie servants in a graveyard. In Haitian folklore, zombies were used as slave labor on plantations. This represented a fate worse than death, as zombies had no free will.

attacked by one. Being robbed of one's free will and forced to do the bidding of another is a frightening notion, especially in places like Haiti, where slavery once flourished.

I AM LEGEND

While traditional voodoo zombies certainly influenced George Romero and the filmmakers who followed him, the most important

This is a scene from 1964's *The Last Man on Earth*. Based on Richard Matheson's book *I Am Legend* and starring horror film legend Vincent Price, *The Last Man on Earth* was the first adaptation of *I Am Legend* for the screen. It was remade in 1971 as *The Omega Man* with Charlton Heston playing the lead.

source for the modern zombie film was Richard Matheson's novel *I Am Legend* (1954). Matheson, a veteran horror writer and screenwriter, constructed a tale about a biological plague that spreads all over the world. In the story, society has been completely destroyed, and human beings have been turned into savage, almost mindless vampires. The only person who has not been affected by the plague is the story's main character, a man named Robert Neville. Neville, like the characters in *Night of the Living Dead*, is not a mythic hero. He is just a normal man.

During the day, he has the world all to himself, but every night, he must defend his home from the creatures who used to be his friends and neighbors. Neville continues on like this, fighting not only the creatures, but also his own despair and loneliness, until he is finally captured by the new society of the vampires and put to death.

For *Night of the Living Dead* and its sequels, Romero replaced vampires with undead flesh-eaters, but the basic elements of *I Am Legend* are all in place. The despair and hopelessness of Romero's zombie films, the total destruction of human soci-

Baron Samedi, the voodoo god of death, is rumored to have been a real voodoo priest whose legend grew over the years. He is often pictured with a long black coat and black hat.

ety, the constant defense against the relentless living dead, the everyman hero, former loved ones turning into horrific enemies, and the ongoing struggle for survival are all borrowed from Matheson's book.

While two films have been made directly from *I Am Legend*, *The Last Man on Earth* (1964) and *The Omega Man* (1971),

Night of the Living Dead could be said to be closer to its spirit than either of them. The potent combination of *I Am Legend*'s themes with images from voodoo tradition has since led to scores of terrifying zombie films, and *Night of the Living Dead* is the father of them all.

CHAPTER 4

CHILDREN OF THE DEAD

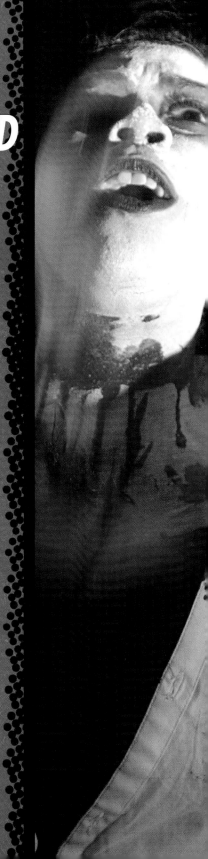

Zombies have been on-screen almost as long as movies have existed. While *Night of the Living Dead* is the best-known zombie movie, it was by no means the first. That distinction goes to a film called *White Zombie* (1932).

Directed by Victor Halperin, *White Zombie* features zombies under the control of an evil voodoo master named Legendre, who is played by the legendary *Dracula* star Bela Lugosi. The zombies are basically just human beings in a trance, and Legendre uses them as slave labor in his mill. Despite being very dated and featuring some poor acting, *White Zombie* is considered one of the few pre–*Night of the Living Dead* zombie movies worthy of note.

I WALKED WITH A ZOMBIE

Another early zombie film was Jacques Tourneur's 1943 film *I Walked with a Zombie*. *I Walked with a Zombie* was a Val Lewton production. Lewton was one of the most successful producers of horror movies in the 1940s. He was responsible for eerie, atmospheric films like

White Zombie (1932) is considered to be the first zombie film ever made. Unlike later zombie films that dealt with decaying, mindless cannibals acting independently, *White Zombie* featured zombies under the control of voodoo master Legendre, played by Bela Lugosi.

Cat People (1942) and was known for his imaginative use of small budgets. With a few dollars, a good story, and a skilled director (such as Tourneur), Lewton was able to make fine, intelligent horror films.

I Walked with a Zombie is very loosely based on Charlotte Brontë's novel *Jane Eyre*. In the film, a nurse travels to the West Indies to look after a wealthy plantation owner's catatonic wife. It is eventually revealed that the woman is not ill but has been turned into a zombie through voodoo ceremonies. Far removed from the savagery of Romero's zombies, the scares in *I Walked with a Zombie* come from skillful use of light, shadow, and sound effects, rather than from violence and gore.

ZOMBIES IN THE 1950s AND 1960s

In the 1950s, voodoo and sorcery no longer seemed scary when compared to the scientific horrors of the atomic bomb. Now, instead of a voodoo priest, movie zombies were often controlled by mad scientists or aliens. In films such as Ed Wood's *Plan 9 from Outer Space* (often considered to be one of the worst films ever made), aliens reanimate corpses to use as an army of conquest against Earth.

This fascination with science and outer space continued into the 1960s, when low-budget drive-in favorites like *Astro Zombies* (1967) presented more aliens and scientists forcing the dead to do their bidding. It was in this atmosphere of silliness that Romero brought out the earth-shattering *Night of the Living Dead*. For once, the dead were under no one's control and had come back to life for no good reason.

In the wake of the massive success of *Night of the Living Dead*, the new style of zombie began to creep its way to the screen, with films like Bob Clark's *Children Shouldn't Play with Dead Things* (1973). But it was Romero again who really got the zombie ball rolling again with his second living dead film, *Dawn of the Dead* (1979).

This is a scene from *Plan 9 from Outer Space* (1956). Directed by the infamous Ed Wood, *Plan 9 from Outer Space* is often called the worst movie ever made. Here, a corpse reanimated by alien scientists turns on his creators. In keeping with the 1950s fixation on science, these zombies were controlled by alien technology instead of voodoo priests.

DAWN OF A NEW ERA

Dawn of the Dead is a sequel to *Night of the Living Dead*. It picks up the story at a point where the zombies have started outnumbering the living. Isolated posses are no longer enough to stem the tide of flesh-eaters, and society is breaking down rapidly. The story follows four survivors as they flee to an abandoned shopping mall and chronicles their attempt at creating a normal life under the constant threat of the living dead.

Filmed in color, *Dawn of the Dead* intensifies the mild gore and makeup effects of its predecessors. The talented makeup artist Tom Savini created grisly and realistic wounds for the zombies. Whereas most of the creatures in *Night of the Living Dead* are simply pale and move stiffly, the zombies in *Dawn of the Dead* are rotting and bleeding.

While the bulk of the film portrays a more successful group of survivors than in *Night of the Living Dead*, it does not have a happy ending. Ultimately, hopelessness prevails. The survivor's shopping mall sanctuary is invaded by zombies due to the greed of a group of outlaw bikers who crash through the mall's defenses. Humankind, not zombies, becomes the real threat to life and limb. In Romero's films, there is no escape once the dead walk among the living, not even from ourselves.

Dawn of the Dead is considered by many to be as good or better than its predecessor. Its influence was felt immediately after its release, especially in Europe, where a number of Italian directors took the gore and realism of Romero's films and brought it to the next level.

ITALIAN ZOMBIES

In the early 1980s, Italian directors like Lucio Fulci and Lamberto Bava created zombie films that were gruesome and unsettling. Fulci's 1980 film *Zombie* depicts some of the most hair-raising zombie action you are ever likely to see, with one of the hungry creatures even attacking a shark! Fulci went on to make several more zombie pictures, including *City of the Living Dead* (1980) and *The Beyond* (1981).

The Italian zombie explosion continued throughout the 1980s and 1990s with highlights such as Lamberto Bava's *Demons* (1985) and Michelle Soavi's *Dellamorte Dellamore* (1994). *Demons* features an interesting twist on the *Night of the Living Dead* formula, with a group of people trying to survive a zombie attack while trapped in a movie theater. *Dellamorte Dellamore*, starring Rupert Everett, is a unique blend of horror and comedy.

AMERICAN DEAD

By the 1980s, zombies had become one of the most popular subjects for low-budget horror films, and the rise of home video and cable television gave them an ever-growing audience. At the same time, the master was still at it. George Romero tackled the next chapter of his zombie saga with 1985's *Day of the Dead*. By the time *Day of the Dead* takes place, human beings have almost completely been overrun, and the dead rule the land. Isolated bits of the former U.S. government and military struggle to maintain order and figure out a way to reclaim the earth for mankind, but by this time the zombies are inescapable.

At the same time, Romero's former partners Rudy Ricci, Russell Streiner, and John Russo worked with *Alien* (1979) screenwriter Dan O'Bannon on a different kind of sequel to *Night of the Living Dead*. Their film, *Return of the Living Dead* (1985), took elements from *Night of the Living Dead* and revved up the comedy. With gruesome makeup effects and a punk rock attitude, *Return of the Living Dead* set itself apart from the more serious Romero films. The zombies in *Return of the Living Dead* craved human brains and weren't quiet about it. *Return of the Living Dead* was successful and spawned two sequels.

GAMES OF DEATH

By the late 1990s, one section of pop culture that was fully infected by zombie movies was that of video games. *Resident*

THE FUNNY DEAD

Return of the Living Dead was by no means the only zombie comedy. Director Sam Raimi's *The Evil Dead* (1982) and its two sequels, *Evil Dead II: Dead by Dawn* (1987) and *Army of Darkness* (1993), mix horror with slapstick comedy and wild camera work. Lead actor Bruce Campbell became the first zombie-fighting superhero as the chainsaw-wielding Ash.

Drawing from the moody, serious horror of author H. P. Lovecraft's story "Herbert West: Reanimator," director Stuart Gordon made a very funny and bizarre zombie comedy called *Re-Animator* (1985). While the movie had little to do with Lovecraft's story, the film became a massive cult hit.

Similar to *The Evil Dead*, but even more extreme in both its gore and comedy, is director Peter Jackson's *Dead-Alive* (1992). *Dead-Alive* features tons of tasteless zombie gore and gross-out humor. Jackson would later go on to direct the *Lord of the Rings* trilogy. Most recently, the British import *Shaun of the Dead* (2004) delighted audiences with its mixture of dry British humor and pulse-pounding thrills.

In this still from George Romero's *Land of the Dead* (2005), zombies roam the roads outside of what is left of Pittsburgh. In the film, survivors have developed advanced weapons to fight the zombies, such as the armored vehicle pictured here. Even this lethal technology is not enough to stop the armies of the dead.

Evil, for the Sony PlayStation, was perhaps the first video game that could boast scares equal to those of any movie. It proved to be so popular that it led to several sequel games and two feature films. *House of the Dead*, a popular zombie arcade game, was also turned into a movie. What was once an underground phenomenon could suddenly be found in teenagers' living rooms all over the world. The zombie invasion was complete.

THE DEAD HAVE THEIR DAY

By the turn of the century, zombies could be found everywhere. They had always been on the silver screen, but now they were also the subject of video games, music, and comic books. They even appeared in cartoons like *The Simpsons*. Of course, zombies remained as strong a presence as ever in movies. Many young people who had grown up watching zombies on video and cable began making films themselves, and they wanted to put their own stamp on the zombie legend.

One of the most successful and innovative recent zombie films isn't really a zombie film at all. The movie *28 Days Later* (2002) features zombies that are not dead but are living people who have been infected with a brain-destroying virus that leaves them homicidal with rage. The virus also enables them to move incredibly quickly. As in Romero's zombie films, society rapidly breaks down, and small bands of survivors have to contend not only with the "zombies" but also with mankind's own evil impulses.

Another popular zombie film was 2004's sleek, big-budget remake of *Dawn of the Dead*. While Romero had overseen a 1990 remake of *Night of the Living Dead*, he had little to do with this one. Still, it remains true to the spirit of the original, with a larger group of survivors struggling with their new lives in a shopping mall. Like *28 Days Later*, the zombies in the remake of *Dawn of the Dead* move quickly. The intense beginning of the film is ranked among zombie cinema's best sequences, and as remakes go, it is considered one of the better ones.

And since no zombie cinema outbreak would be complete without him, George Romero himself returned with his fourth chapter in the saga of the dead with 2005's *Land of the Dead*. This time, Romero even went as far as to make the zombies seem somewhat heroic, with a greedy tycoon played by Dennis Hopper as the movie's true villain. The zombies, who are now the planet's dominant life-form, spend most of the movie just looking for a home of their own. The living dead have come a long way from their humble beginnings in the Pennsylvania countryside.

FILMOGRAPHY

White Zombie (1932). Perhaps the first zombie film ever made. A wealthy plantation owner longs to lure a young woman away from her fiancé. He uses the services of a devious zombie-controlling mill owner to make her his slave.

I Walked with a Zombie (1943). A young nurse goes to the West Indies to care for a plantation owner's catatonic wife. It turns out that the wife has been made into a zombie through the use of voodoo ceremonies.

Plan 9 from Outer Space (1959). This low-budget Ed Wood film features aliens bent on creating a zombie army of resurrected corpses.

Night of the Living Dead (1968). The blueprint for the modern flesh-eating zombie. A group of people struggle to survive a gruesome assault by hungry walking corpses.

Children Shouldn't Play with Dead Things (1972). A group of actors go to an island to act out a magical ritual. They are shocked when the ritual works and the dead begin to rise.

Dawn of the Dead (1978). George Romero's follow-up to *Night of the Living Dead*. As the living dead begin to take over America, four survivors attempt to hide out in a well-stocked but deserted shopping mall.

Zombie (1979). Italian director Lucio Fulci's gore-soaked zombie film was inspired by *Dawn of the Dead*. It is far more gruesome than its American cousins.

The Evil Dead (1981). Sam Raimi, director of the 2002 film *Spider-Man*, directed this wild, exciting living dead film. *The Evil Dead* mixes slapstick comedy with scares.

Day of the Dead (1985). George Romero's third zombie film. The dead have taken over, and a small military outpost of human beings tries to stay alive while studying the zombies.

Re-Animator (1985). Bizarre zombie comedy loosely based on the writings of H. P. Lovecraft. Student Herbert West arrives at a medical school, where his experiments in reviving the dead cause problems right away.

Return of the Living Dead (1985). *Alien* screenwriter Dan O'Bannon made his directorial debut with this popular zombie comedy. A small town is infested with zombies after a chemical leak at a military storage installation.

Evil Dead II: Dead by Dawn (1987). Raimi's follow-up to *The Evil Dead* is more of a remake than a sequel. Bruce Campbell returns as the heroic Ash, and slapstick madness ensues.

Night of the Living Dead (1990). Makeup wizard Tom Savini's remake of Romero's original is very similar to the first film, but with much-improved makeup.

Dead-Alive (1992). From *Lord of the Rings* director Peter Jackson, this zombie comedy features twisted humor and incredible creature effects. One of the funniest and goriest zombie films ever made.

Army of Darkness (1993). The third and final film in Raimi's *Evil Dead* trilogy. Bruce Campbell travels in time to medieval England to fight the walking dead.

Resident Evil (2002). This zombie film is based on the smash-hit video game of the same name. A special military unit fights an underground lab full of zombies after a virus runs out of control.

28 Days Later (2002). While not technically a zombie movie, this intense English import is very close to one. A virus that infects people with mindless rage quickly spreads across London.

Dawn of the Dead (2004). Well-made remake of the 1978 original. As a worldwide zombie plague turns most people into the living dead, a small group of survivors seek refuge in a shopping mall. This version features more characters and cutting-edge special effects.

Shaun of the Dead (2004). An English zombie comedy about a young man in a dead-end life who is forced to make some positive changes when his town is infested by zombies.

GLOSSARY

cannibal A human being who eats the flesh of other human beings.

catatonic To be in a trancelike state. People who are catatonic are alive, but unable to move or speak.

corpse A dead body.

distributor A company that gets prints of a movie into theaters all over the country.

eerie Subtly frightening or unsettling.

genre A particular classification of something.

gore Graphic scenes of blood and injury in a movie.

homicidal Prepared to commit murder.

investor A person who contributes money for a project, with the intention of making even more money once the project is finished.

maniac A violent, mentally disturbed individual.

premiere To make a first public appearance.

reanimate To bring back to life.

voodoo A religion originating in West Africa and widely practiced on the island of Haiti.

FOR MORE INFORMATION

American Museum of the Moving Image
35th Avenue at 36th Street
Astoria, NY 11106
(718) 784-0077
Web site: http://www.ammi.org

The American Film Institute
2021 Western Avenue
Los Angeles, CA 90027-1657
(323) 856-7600
Web site: http://www.afi.com

WEB SITES

Due to the changing nature of Internet links, the Rosen
Publishing Group, Inc., has developed an online list of Web
sites related to the subject of this book. This site is updated
regularly. Please use this link to access the list:

http://www.rosenlinks.com/famm/zomb

FOR FURTHER READING

Brooks, Max. *The Zombie Survival Guide: Complete Protection from the Living Dead*. London, England: Duckworth, 2004.

Cohen, Daniel. *Horror in the Movies*. New York, NY: Clarion Books, 1982.

Cohen, Daniel. *Raising the Dead*. New York, NY: Cobblehill Books, 1997.

Dendle, Peter. *The Zombie Movie Encyclopedia*. Jefferson, NC: McFarland, 2001

Russell, Jamie. *Book of the Dead: The Complete History of Zombie Cinema*. Surrey, England: Fab Press, 2005.

Skal, David J. *The Monster Show: A Cultural History of Horror*. London, England: Faber & Faber, 2001.

BIBLIOGRAPHY

Cohen, Daniel. *Raising the Dead.* New York, NY: Cobblehill Books, 1997.

Hood, Robert. "Nights of the Celluloid Dead: A History of the Zombie Film." Retrieved July 7, 2005 (http://www.phillyburbs.com/zombies/essay/one.shtml).

Murray, Rebecca. "George Romero Talks About Land of the Dead." Retrieved August 5, 2005 (http://movies.about.com/od/landofthedead/a/deadgr062105.htm).

Powers, Tom. *Horror Movies.* Minneapolis, MN: Lerner Publications, 1989.

Russo, John. *The Complete Night of the Living Dead Film Book.* New York, NY: Harmony Books, 1985.

Slater, Jay. *Eaten Alive! Italian Cannibal and Zombie Movies.* London, England: Plexus Publishing, 2002.

INDEX

ABOUT THE AUTHOR

Thomas Forget has been studying horror cinema since before he could read. He first became fascinated by movie monsters while watching *Creature Double Feature* on Saturdays as a child. He currently lives in Brooklyn, NY.

PHOTO CREDITS

Cover Variety/The Kobal Collection; pp. 4, 14, 24, 31 © Ramin Talaie/Corbis; pp. 5, 9, 28, 32, 34 Everett Collection; pp. 7, 10, 17, 20 Photofest; p. 19 © Bettman/Corbis; p. 22 Getty Images; p. 25 © Philip Gould/Corbis; p. 27 The Art Archive/Haitian Art Museum, Port au Prince/Mireille Vautier; p. 29 courtesy Indigo Arts Gallery; p. 38 © Michael Gibson/Universal Pictures/ZUMA/Corbis.

Designer: Thomas Forget